To Hank van Oss '39,

On the occasion of your retirement as chairman of the Alumni Council Committee on Academic Programs for Alumni, I hope you will accept this book as a token of our special thanks for the leadership you have given in establishing the Alumni Colleges as a vital link between the University and alumni.

Bill Bowen
April 27, 1984

PRINCETON REFLECTIONS

PRINCETON

REFLECTIONS

Contemplations in Color

PRINCETON UNIVERSITY PRESS

Library of Congress Cataloging in Publication Data

Campbell, Bruce, 1946–
Princeton reflections.
1. Princeton University — Description — Pictorial
works. I. Title.
LD4611.C35 1982   378.749'67   82-47902
ISBN 0-691-03974-7

"It still has the look, and the feel, of an institution deliberately designed for 'thinking' and kept that way down all its years."

LEWIS THOMAS, 1981

Introduction

The face of Princeton is ever changing. It grows older, with character and with grace; and it grows younger, as new features rise to dot its landscape. As the home of one of the world's great universities, the campus has no choice but to change.

And yet there is something unchanging about Princeton. The words and pictures of earlier times may seem quaint, but they strike a responsive chord. While any effort to freeze the image forever is doomed to failure, there is something enduring that can be captured.

This book endeavors to capture that something for this generation. It is designed for those who know Princeton now and those who shall come to know her, including those of posterity who will turn to these pages in their time to assuage their curiosities about what has come before them.

For nearly half a century, Nassau Hall housed the entire College of New Jersey. But over the next two hundred years, through its evolution into a university of world renown, Princeton expanded in many ways. It now covers more than two thousand acres, of which roughly two hundred comprise the main campus. A wealth of architectural styles is displayed, ranging from the oldest colonial buildings to the predominantly Gothic dormitories, and including modern structures by such eminent architects as

Opposite: Stone vaulting on the eastern entrance to Holder Courtyard. Photo by John W.H. Simpson.

Minoru Yamasaki, Edward Larrabee Barnes, Robert Venturi, and I.M. Pei. Interspersed throughout the campus are arresting outdoor sculptures, and enough notable trees to constitute a modest arboretum.

The campus is home to approximately forty-five hundred undergraduates and fifteen hundred graduate students in some sixty departments and programs. Serving these students are dormitories and academic buildings housing classrooms, laboratories, libraries, and museums, as well as athletic facilities generally considered to be among the finest in the nation. Juxtaposed along one of Princeton's central plazas is one of the world's most majestic college chapels and one of the world's finest and most handsome research libraries.

The impressions that Princeton makes on the mind and memory are no doubt as varied as the individuals on whom they are made. But they seem to be vivid and long-lasting, whether the individual has been a student, a faculty or staff member, a resident of the community, or a visitor.

The most immediate impression for many is the physical beauty of the campus. As early as 1766, in a letter notifying John Witherspoon of his election as president, Trustee William Peartree Smith boasted that "the Situation of the College is in a very populous, agreeable & healthy Country, upon an elevated tract of

Ground, in a clear and wholesome Air: the latter appears from the uncommon state of Health which hath always been remarkable among the Students & Inhabitants of the Village."

Following a visit to the campus over a century later, Moses Taylor Pyne, a member of the Class of 1877 and a generous Princeton benefactor, recorded that the campus looked "simply exquisite...I never saw an English lawn kept in better shape, and the great elms and beautiful buildings rising out of the rich turf make a beautiful picture."

Returning to his alma mater for an honorary degree in 1899, Basil L. Gildersleeve, a member of the Class of 1849 and a scholar who had dominated American classical studies for fifty years, remarked that two features of the campus "remain essentially the same: the elms, like some of the Class of '49, have increased in girth, but they are still glorious in their greenery; and the cannon, about which the young spirits of Princeton have revolved for generations, still keeps its adamantine lips discreetly sealed."

V. Lansing Collins, of the Class of 1892, an historian of the University, noted among Princetonians a "pride of ownership," a "sense of belonging" that led them to assume personal responsibility for the continuing beauty of the campus. Their affection and generosity can be seen and admired in the form of buildings, gardens, trees, and playing fields throughout the campus. They are found also in less visible form at the very heart of the University in its professorships, fellowships, and scholarships, and in its various other endowment funds.

This concentration of physical, human, and financial resources has helped to make Princeton one of the world's premiere institutions of higher learning and research. As Princeton's seventeenth president, William G. Bowen, observed: "The only justification for the great resources at the disposal of Princeton University, in the form of a remarkable collection of people as well as excellent facilities, is that quality matters."

Quality does matter — in the buildings and landscapes that provide our initial impressions, and in the teaching and scholarly activity that, on a more fundamental level, are why this campus exists. This commitment to quality is pervasive and persistent, and it leaves a most indelible impression upon those who come in contact with it.

Another of Princeton's characteristics is its deep concern for the individual, a concern that finds expression through the University's avowedly residential nature as well as through its academic programs. An institution of high achievement, it is also a place that engenders powerful feelings of community, of association, and of obligation to be of service to others.

Out of this environment arises a unique loyalty, and out of that loyalty respect, and out of that respect responsibility. This sense of personal responsibility, seen so clearly in the relationships between Princetonians and their alma mater, is seen also in their leadership in community, national, and international life.

Another attribute of Princeton's personality, its emphasis on fundamental knowledge in the central core of the arts and sciences, has contributed to an enviable orderliness and harmony in its institutional structure. Emanating from this structure, with its single faculty and its well-integrated relationships among faculty, students, administrators, and trustees, is an ambiance of restraint at Princeton that has spared this University from undisciplined expansion and has encouraged a seeking of excellence within carefully determined bounds.

Integral to this ambiance is a basic style once described by J. Douglas Brown, Princeton's first provost and long-time dean of the faculty, as "a blending of intellectual, aesthetic, and emotional elements in a desire for more perfect expression, for elegance with economy, for precision without dullness, and for lift without blatancy. A sense of style shifts the focus from being better than someone else to attaining the best expression of one's self through creative insight and intelligence."

This volume seeks to capture both the beauty and the style of Princeton. In doing so, it carries us through the seasons of the academic year, through "Contemplations in Color" selected by

Bruce Campbell from the work of more than a dozen photographers. It need hardly be said that no collection of this size could provide a comprehensive record of modern-day Princeton. It is hoped, nonetheless, that these artistic reflections will bring a full measure of aesthetic appreciation and pleasure to all who know and care for Princeton.

It is hoped also that the beauty revealed through these pages will encompass far more than just the vistas and the surface features of this famous campus, as captivating as they are. Inevitably what is emphasized here will be architecture and landscape. But good architecture and landscape design express the inner purposes of structures and their arrangement. There is a rare and compelling beauty in the effort to understand, in the search for truth, in the striving for excellence. It is hoped that those who peruse these pages will find that beauty, and in it the real meanings of this University.

Opposite: Stone vaulting on the eastern entrance to Holder Courtyard. Photo by John W.H. Simpson.

"Who can calculate the rich revenue of honor and glory it will ere long bring to this nation and to the world?" DANIEL NEWELL, 1832

1

3

4

5

8

9

10

11

12

13

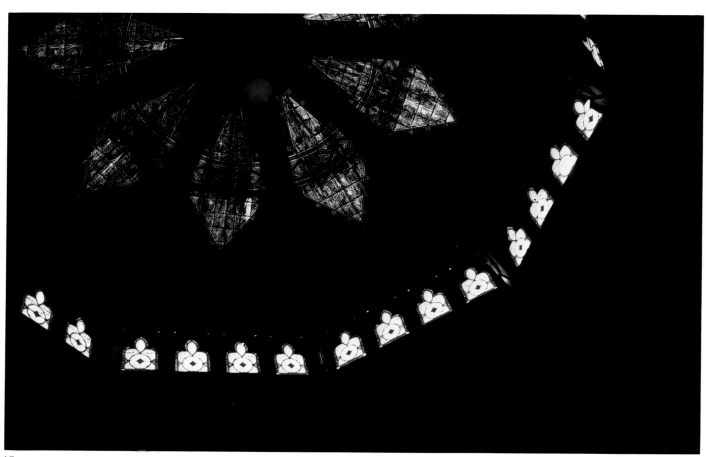

15

18

19

20

21

" . . . the great elms and beautiful buildings
rising out of the rich turf make a beautiful picture."

MOSES TAYLOR PYNE, 1877

23

24

25

26

29

34

35

40

" . . . the beauty of the place haunts the recollections of Princeton poets and novelists."

V. LANSING COLLINS, 1932

41

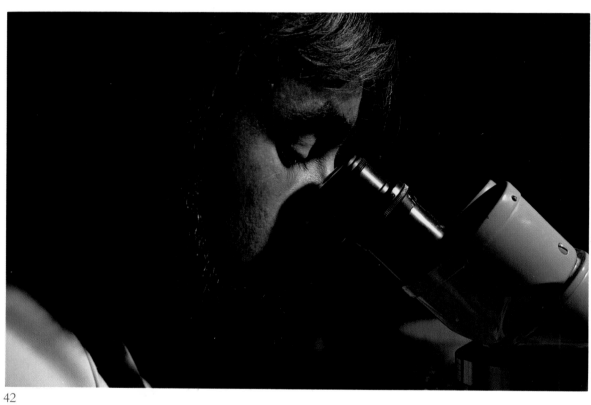

42

43

44

47

48

49

50

51

52

53

54

56

57

59

"We drove a little through the campus, after dusk. It was soft, the air fresh, the beginning of spring." ADLAI E. STEVENSON, 1954

61

62

63

65

66

68

71

72

73

74

77

78

Design and Photo Selection: *Bruce Campbell Design*
Typesetting: *D8TATEXT+*
Typeface: *Display/Augustea; Text/Bembo*
Text Printing: *Princeton University Press*
Stock: *80 lb. Curtis Tweedweave Text*
Color Printing: *Princeton Polychrome Press*
Stock: *100 lb. Vintage Velvet Text*
Binder: *American Book-Stratford Press, Inc.*
Binding Cloth: *Holliston Zeppelin*